STILL MORE OF

The World's Best Dirty Jokes

Mr. "J"

CASTLE

This edition published by Castle, a division of Book Sales, Inc. Re-printed by special permission of Citadel Press (a division of Lyle Stuart, Inc.)

ISBN 0-89009-586-8

Manufactured in the United States of America

10 9 8 7 6 5 4 3 2 1

Foreword

No gentleman has ever heard a story before.
ANON.

This is the third and final volume of Mr. "J" 's collections of the world's best dirty jokes. Reader reaction to the first two collections, *The World's Best Dirty Jokes* and *More of the World's Best Dirty Jokes,* was so positive that the author again searched his vast storehouse of material for jokes and stories worthy of inclusion.

Some of the jokes and stories are new; some you may have read (or heard) in different versions. Most of them might merit being X-rated. But we believe you and your friends can pick up this book and enjoy hours of smiles, chuckles and plain old belly laughs.

"Laughter is the most inexpensive and most effective wonder drug Laughter is a universal medicine "
BERTRAND RUSSELL

Three coeds were talking about a guy each had dated during the past few weeks.

The first said, "He thinks he's pretty sophisticated, so I decided to teach him a lesson. When I went to his room I found his condoms lying on the table. I stuffed them into one of his socks so he couldn't find them and, boy, did that cramp his style."

The second girl said, "I thought that a sock was a peculiar place to keep rubbers. But I really took care of him. Since it was my period, I didn't worry about getting laid, but I did take the rubbers and punctured each one and put them back in the drawer where he could find them."

The third coed fainted.

An Englishman, a Pole and a Puerto Rican were standing atop the Empire State building, bemoaning their respective fates. Disgusted with their lives the three formed a suicide pact.

The Briton jumped first, sailing neatly to his doom . . . the Pole got lost on the way down . . . and the Puerto Rican stopped every few floors to scribble "Fuck you!" on the walls.

Two couples who had been great friends since they had gotten married decided to share a Rocky Mountain vacation.

They pitched two tents and cooked their dinners over a roaring campfire. Ample supplies of booze made the food tastier.

When it came bedtime, one of the men asked the other three: "What do you think of all this switching around that's going on?"

The question excited the others, and they decided to experiment.

After a few hours, the man turned to his new bedmate and said, "I haven't had such a great time in years. Do you think the girls are having as much fun as we are?"

An inexperienced young man, prior to his wedding, asked his father how to conduct himself.

"Well," said the father, "you take the thing you used to play with when you were a teenager and put it where your wife wee-wees."

So the young man took his baseball and threw it in the toilet.

An airplane passenger, being served drinks by the stewardess, exclaimed: "Hey, here's something new ... an ice cube with a hole in it!"

"What's new about that?" answered the man sitting alongside. "I married one."

A traveling salesman, completing a trip earlier than anticipated, sent his wife a telegram: "Returning home Friday."

Arriving home, he found his wife in bed with another man. Being a person of non-violence, he complained to his father-in-law, who said, "I'm sure there must be an explanation."

The next day the father-in-law was all smiles. "I knew there was an explanation. She didn't get your telegram."

A reporter asked the great artist Picasso why he tolerated the sexual escapades of his much younger wife. "Well," said the artist, "I'd rather have 20% of a growing concern than a 100% interest in a bankruptcy."

What do they call a Chinese voyeur?
A Peiping Tom.

Silas and Sally were in the cornfield behind the barn, happily fucking away.

It had rained a lot that day and the earth was muddy. The bare-assed couple were slipping around a good deal.

Silas became concerned. "Say, honey," he asked, "is my cock in you or is it in the mud?"

Sally felt down and said, "Why, honey, it's in the mud."

"Well, put it back in you," Silas sighed.

Things seemed to be going okay, but Silas still had his doubts.

"Say, honey, is it in you or in the mud?"

"Why, Silas, it's in me," Sally cooed happily.

"Well, put it back in the mud."

While dancing at Roseland, a man assayed small talk with his partner. "Honey, do you know the minuet?"

"Hell, no," she replied, "I don't even know the men I've laid."

The aged patient toddered into the doctor's office with a serious complaint.

"Doc, you've got to do something to lower my sex drive."

"Come on now, Mr. Peters," the dostor said, "your sex drive's all in your head."

"That's what I mean; you've got to lower it a little."

Not in Webster's Dictionary: Definition of a gynecologist as a spreader of old wives' tales.

LITTLE BOY: "Mama, where do babies come from?"
MAMA: "From the stork, of course."
LITTLE BOY: "But, Mama, who fucks the stork?"

How do you make Manischewitz wine?
Squeeze his balls!

Frank and Ronald—a married-without-benefit-of-clergy homosexual couple—had been spending a quiet evening at home.

"Hey, Ronald," Frank called out, "has the paper boy come yet?"

"Not yet, but he's getting a glassy look in his eyes."

RECENT GRAFFITI IN THE MEN'S WASHROOMS

The crying crabs . . . it crawls up your legs and bawls. Stand up close to the urinal . . . the next guy may be barefoot.

If you sprinkle when you tinkle . . . be a sweetie and wipe the seatie.

Hey, Bud, stand up closer . . . you've got a pistol in your hand, not a Winchester.

Chuck was always shy with girls.

One evening, he got his best friend, Bob, to go with him to a singles bar. Bob, being very experienced, was supposed to help Chuck in his quest for female companionship, and sexual companionship.

One sweet young thing in the room noticed Chuck, thought he was cute, and decided to make contact with him. Since she was a little shy, she could not just go up to him, but had to use gestures.

"Bob," Chuck said. "That girl over there is giving me the eye. What should I do?"

"Give her the eye back," replied Bob.

So Chuck, as best as he could, gave her the eye.

A few moments passed.

"Bob," said Chuck, now getting rather excited. "She's smiling at me. What do I do?"

"Smile back," was the reply.

So Chuck, trying to appear cool and calm, smiled back

A few more moments passed.

"Bob! ! !" exclaimed Chuck. "My God. She bent over and showed me her tits. Now what do I do?"

"Show her your nuts," Bob calmly replied.

So Chuck turned toward the girl, stuck his thumbs in his ears, and waving his fingers stuck out his tongue, and wiggling it, exclaimed, "Bluble, bluble, bluble!"

Two soldiers were canvassing the streets in a new town when a girl popped out of a doorway and cried: "Hey, fellows, come on in and I'll give you something you've never had before."

One soldier grabbed the other's arm and said, "Let's get the hell out of here. She's got leprosy."

Two buddies at the bar, drinking away, were comparing the sexual behavior of their spouses.

"Hey," one asked, "does your wife close her eyes when you're pumping away on her?"

"She sure does," replied the other. "She just can't stand to watch me having a good time."

Millie was complaining to Janis that her latest lover only wants to "eat it."

Janis said, "You're a lucky girl, but if you want to discourage him, why not rub garlic in your pussy?"

"I tried that," said Millie, "but the next night he came to bed with some lettuce and olive oil."

The woman had been away for two days visiting a sick friend in another city. When she returned, her little boy greeted her by saying, "Mommy, guess what! Yesterday I was playing in the closet in your bedroom and Daddy came into the room with the lady next door and they got undressed and got into your bed and then Daddy got on top of her————"

Sonny's mother held up her hand. "Not another word. Wait till your father comes home and then I want you to tell him exactly what you've just told me."

The father came home. As he walked into the house, his wife said, "I'm leaving you. I'm packing now and I'm leaving you."

"But why————" asked the startled father.

"Go ahead, Sonny. Tell Daddy just what you told me."

"Well," Sonny said, "I was playing in your bedroom closet and Daddy came upstairs with the lady next door and they got undressed and got into bed and Daddy got on top of her and then they did just what you did with Uncle John when Daddy was away last summer."

A guy had his male cat "fixed" because he was a menace to the neighborhood, sneaking out at night and impregnating all the neighbors' female cats.

The tom still sneaks out at night . . but now he acts as a consultant.

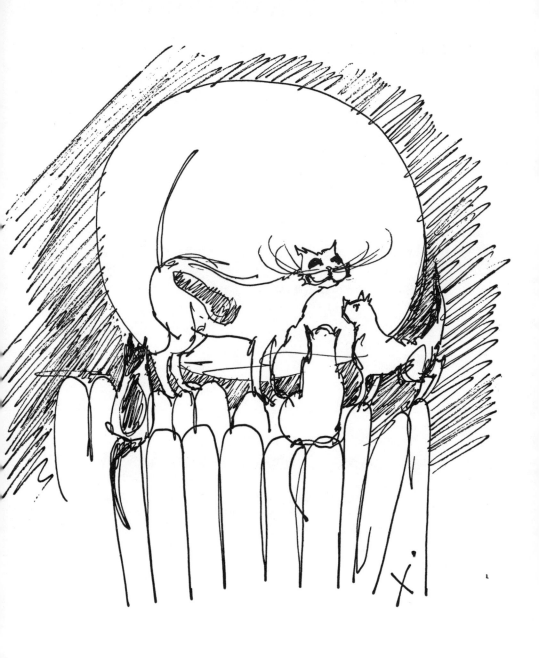

Overheard at a cocktail party: A husband was asking his wife, "Tell me, dear, before we married, did you say you were oversexed or over sex?"

FIRST DRUNK: "My wife is an angel."
SECOND DRUNK: "You're lucky . . . my wife is still alive!"

A disappointed father, expecting a son, complained to the doctor that he was anticipating a baby with a penis.

"Yes," said the doctor, "but just imagine that in about eighteen years, she'll have a beautiful place to put one in."

There was an old man from Nantucket
Whose cock was so long
He could suck it.
He said, with a grin,
As he wiped off his chin:
If my ear was a cunt,
I could fuck it!

Two men sitting side by side were having their respective scalps tonsured. The first barber asked his client if he'd like some French toilet water on his hair.

"Oh, no," the man said. "My wife would think I'd been in a French whorehouse."

The second barber asked the same question of his client, who said, "Why, sure, my wife has never been in a French whorehouse."

n unfortunate young man was thrown out of the Boy Scouts for eating Brownies.

Little William went to his father and said, "Daddy, where did I come from?"

The father started to stutter and stammer, but he realized that he had to tell his son the facts of life.

"Sit down, Willie," he said.

At great length, he described the whole business of creation, beginning with the birds and the bees. Then he went into the most graphic descriptions of human intercourse.

He concluded at last, feeling limp and drained. He took a kerchief and wiped the perspiration from his brow. "Okay, Willie, do you understand now?"

Willie scratched his head. "Not really, Dad. Henry says he came from New Jersey but you haven't told me where I come from."

A man and his attractive companion were enjoying a cocktail party where one of the other female guests was expounding her philosophy. "I guess I'm just an animal," she was saying, "all I want to do is sleep and make love." The man's companion agreed, "I sleep and make love too."

"Yes," the man said, "but do you do both at the same time!"

Pole was suffering from constipation, so his doctor prescribed suppositories.

A week later the Pole complained to the doctor that they didn't produce the desired results.

"Have you been taking them regularly?" the doctor asked.

"What do you think I've been doing," the Pole said, "shoving them up my ass?"

A pigeon invited his friends to the top of the World Trade Center in New York. As he flew past the observation deck he answered a call of nature. The other pigeons watched as his droppings floated gracefully to the street.

"See, fellows," the pigeon said, "a little shit goes a long way in this town."

The little Jewish man was sitting on a bench at Atlantic City saying, "They're wonderful! They're marvelous! They're magnificent!"

A policeman sauntered over to him. "What are you talking about, me lad?"

The man on the bench replied: "I've just been reading history. That Israeli army—look how they beat those Arabs."

The cop said, "Fuck the Israeli army!"

The man on the bench looked a little aghast. "Well, take the late Prime Minister, Golda Meir. Didn't she run things well? What a woman she was!"

The cop said, "Fuck Golda Meir!"

The man on the bench thought for a minute and then said, "Well, take the way those immigrants have taken a barren desert and built it—"

The cop said, "Fuck those immigrants and their barren desert!"

The little man stared up at the cop. "Excuse me, officer. What nationality are you?"

"What do you think I am? I'm Irish, of course."

And the man on the bench said, "Fuck Ella Fitzgerald!"

37

A man went to a plastic surgeon to get work done on his penis.

The doctor, curious, asked what had happened to it.

"Well," the patient said, "I live in a trailer camp. A gorgeous buxom creature lives in the trailer next to mine. I used to peek into her trailer and I saw that she had a habit. Each afternoon she'd take a frankfurter from her refrigerator and put it in a hole on her trailer floor. Then she'd sit on it and have a ball.

"She nearly drove me crazy. So I got a bright idea. One day I got under her trailer and when she slid the frankfurter into the hole, I slid it out and slipped my cock up through the hole.

"She sat down on it and everything was going just great until there was a knock at the door."

"And then?" said the doctor.

"Aw hell," the patient explained. "That's when she tried to kick it under the stove."

A gay guy used to hang out in the neighborhood drugstore, where the gang always greeted him by saying, "Hello, cunt."

The homosexual never reacted. One day, however, after the usual "Hello, cunt" greeting, the gay said vehemently: "Don't you call me that!"

"Why not?" the head of the gang wanted to know.

"Because," he lisped, "the other day I saw one."

Little Gwen opened the back door to the kitchen where her mother was cooking dinner.

"Mom," she asked, "can a nine-year-old girl become pregnant?"

"Of course not," her mother said.

Gwen turned around. "Okay, fellows," she called, "let's continue playing the game."

D oreen was in bed, anxiously waiting for her date to take off his pants. When he did and she saw the size of his organ, she jumped out of bed and ran to the desk drawer.

"What the hell are you doing?" he cried.

"I'm getting a crayon," she said. "You've got to draw the line somewhere."

An armless man walked into John's Bar and ordered a beer. When served, he asked the bartender to help him drink it by holding the glass. This was done cheerfully and then repeated twice. After the third beer, the customer asked the location of the men's room. The bartender pointed to the rear of the bar but intoned sternly, "You go there, alone."

Four men had played golf together for two years. At the conclusion of the games, three of the men always showered together and then had a few drinks at the bar. The fourth man would hurry home.

One day one of the trio asked the fourth man, "Listen, how come you never stick around?"

The fourth man was uncomfortable. "All right, I'll tell you. I don't stay because I don't want to shower with you. I'm embarrassed because my penis is very small."

The other man asked, "Does it work?"

"Sure, it works very well."

"Well how would you like to trade it for one that looks good in the shower?"

The recently married bride was perplexed when her husband announced that he had found a new position.

"What's that, honey?"

"We lie back to back."

"But, what kind of position is that?"

"You'll see. Another couple is joining us."

My friend was telling a pal that he had a dream that he was alone in a boat with Dolly Parton. His pal asked, "Really, how did you make out?" My friend said, "Great, I caught a twelve-pound bass."

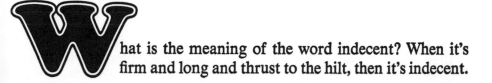hat is the meaning of the word indecent? When it's firm and long and thrust to the hilt, then it's indecent.

 divorcee took an office job and said. "I hope I'll find sexual harassment on the job."

Two kids were having the standard argument about whose father could beat up whose father.

One boy said, "My father is better than your father."

The other kid said, "Well, my mother is better than your mother."

The first boy paused, "I guess you're right. My father says the same thing."

An old gentleman slowly approached the local brothel and pressed the doorbell.

The madam opened the door, looked at the old fellow with a critical eye and then asked: "What can we do for you, sir?"

"I need a girl," the senior citizen said.

"For you, the charge is a hundred dollars."

"You're putting me on," he exclaimed.

"That will be an extra ten dollars," said the madam.

An important executive was telling friends at his country club about some of his experiences. "So I bought this yacht that could carry fifty people and I took it out for a maiden voyage and it hit a reef and sunk.

"Then I bought an airplane and on the first flight it hit another plane on the field and it burned up.

"Then I married this beautiful blonde and no sooner did I get home than I found her fooling around with the chauffeur and I had to divorce her."

"So what's the moral?" one of the others asked.

"Clear as a bell," said the old man. "If it swims, flies or fucks, lease it, don't buy it."

wo elderly priests and a young novitiate wanted to buy train tickets to Pittsburgh at a railway station. The young girl selling tickets was pretty and endowed with a large and shapely set of breasts, set off by a V-neck that displayed her mammaries to great advantage every time she bent forward.

The young novitiate approached the ticket booth and said, "Miss, please give me three tickets to Tittsville."

"How dare you?" remonstrated the ticket seller.

The first priest said, "Let me handle this. Miss," he stammered, "three pickets to Tittsburgh, please, and give me the change in nipples and dimes."

The second priest, the eldest of the trio, tried to placate the angry young woman.

"Three tickets to Pittsburgh, please, and you should dress more decorously, young woman, or Saint Finger is going to point his peter at you!"

Someone left the zebra's cage open in the middle of the night and he escaped and ran away to a local farm.

Early the next morning, he approached an old hen, saying, "What do you do around here?"

The hen replied, "I lay eggs for the farmer's breakfast."

The zebra then walked over to the cow, asking, "What do you do?"

The cow replied, "I give milk for the farmer's breakfast."

The zebra then spied an enormous bull and asked the same question.

The bull looked at the zebra with a quizzical smile and said: "Listen, you queer ass, take off those faggy pajamas and I'll show you what I do around here."

It was the first Christmas and the first of the Three Wise Men slowly approached the barn and gingerly crossed over the threshold—into a big juicy pile of horse shit.

Looking down at his gold slippers, he let out a shriek— "Je-sus Christ!"

The woman at the manger turned to her companion and said, "Joseph, that's a better name for the kid than Irving."

The henpecked husband was asked why he couldn't bear to sit through porno movies.

"I can't stand one guy enjoying himself more in ten minutes than I have in the last twenty years."

NOT IN MOTHER GOOSE RHYMES

Y stands for Yanker,
The self-driving chap.
He greases his pole and
Provokes his own sap.

Absolved of the need of
A quarrelsome wife,
He humps himself nightly
And lives a great life.

Three women were bragging about what great husbands they married.

The first said, "My husband is fantastic. He bought me two mink coats and an ermine wrap."

The second said, "My husband bought me two sailboats and also a yacht that twelve people can live on."

"My husband is poor," said the third woman, "but you can have your rich husbands with their fur coats and their yachts. My husband is very special. He has a penis so long that thirteen birds can stand on it side by side."

There was a long silence. The first woman said, "Listen, I was lying to you. My husband didn't get me all those fancy coats. He bought me one small cloth coat at Alexanders and I'm very happy with it."

The second woman said, "Well, since we're telling the truth, you might as well know I didn't get two sailboats and a fancy yacht. All I got was a rowboat ride in Central Park."

Both women turned and stared at the third.

"Okay, okay!" she said. "So I'll tell the truth too. The business about the thirteen birds who can stand side by side on my husband's penis is not true. The thirteenth bird can only stand on one leg."

The tough character was mumbling to his friend, "My girl, Mary, is going to die of syphilis."

"No," the friend said, "people don't die of syphilis anymore."

"They do when they give it to me!" was the rejoinder.

A businessman who had his life savings wiped out in the market came home and told his wife, "Honey, I'm absolutely busted, penniless. We have to start all over again."

The wife shuddered, saying, "I can't change my way of life; I'd rather be dead." And with that she leaped out of the open window.

The newly widowed husband smiled: "Thank you, Paine, Webber . . ."

A fellow has a girlfriend whose bedroom is done entirely in mirrors: walls, ceiling, the whole bit. When he calls on her he brings along a bottle of Ajax Window Cleaner.

CENSORED MOTHER GOOSE

I

Charley loves good cake and ale;
Charley loves good candy;
Charley loves to——— the girls—
When they are clean and handy.

II

See-saw, Margaret Daw,
Jenny shall have a new master;
She shall have but a penny a day
Because she can't——— any faster.

Sam was very worried. His teenage daughter was hitch-hiking home from Miami to Minneapolis by herself. She was seventeen but was built like she was twenty-five. When she arrived home unscathed her father was curious as to how she avoided rape, if not worse.

"I simply told all the men who picked me up that I was going to the clinic in Minneapolis because it's the number one establishment in the country for curing V.D." she replied sweetly.

Through the first four holes in the golf course, Jim was very quiet. Finally, on the fifth tee, John asked, "What the hell's the matter, Jim? You're so silent."

"It's my wife, Ann," John replied. "Ever since she's been working overtime at the phone company, she's cut our sex down to twice a week."

"You're lucky," replied John. "She's cut me off completely."

So this old man went to his doctor.
"I've got toilet problems," he complained.
"Well, let's see. How is your urination?"
"Every morning at seven o'clock like a baby."
"Good. How about your bowel movement?"
"Eight o'clock each morning like clockwork."
"So what's the problem?" the doctor asked.
"I don't wake up until nine!"

There once was a girl from Jahore
Who'd lie on a rug on the floor.
In a manner uncanny, she'd wiggle her fanny
And drain your balls dry to the core.

There once was a lady from France
Who took a long train ride by chance.
The engineer fucked her before the conductor
While the fireman came in his pants.

A young man in love with a girl he wanted to fuck was so ashamed of his small penis that he was afraid of bringing up the question, or of letting her see him naked.

One dark night he drove her around in his car and parked in a dark lane. As they kissed he surreptitiously opened his fly and put his weapon in her hand.

"Thanks," she said. "But you know I don't smoke."

A patient, suffering from an impacted wisdom tooth, went to his dentist.

"That tooth has got to be pulled immediately," the dentist said as he reached for a wicked-looking set of forceps.

The patient reached out and got a tight grip on the dentist's balls. "We're not going to hurt each other, are we, doctor?"

The census taker asked a girl to give her occupation.
"Whore," she answered.
"I can't list it that way, Miss."
"Okay, put down prostitute."
"I can't list it that way either."
"How about chicken raiser?"
"Chicken raiser?" he asked in puzzlement.
"Sure, last year I raised nine hundred cocks."

Charlie was telling his tale of woe to his boss. He said, "I was so drunk last night that I don't know how I got home. Not realizing it was my bed I slept in when I awoke, I handed the woman next to me a $20 bill."

"Is that what's making you sad?"

"No," said Charlie. "It was my wife I gave the $20 to, but she gave me $10 change."

Maw told her son Clem to check out the family out-door one-holer.

"Tain't nothin' wrong with it, Maw," Clem insisted. But she took him out to the outhouse and made him stick his head down inside the hole.

"Maw," he called from the depths, "my beard's stuck!"

"Aggravatin', ain't it?" said Maw.

MORE CENSORED MOTHER GOOSE

I

Bobby Shafto's gone to sea;
Silver buckles on his knee;
When he comes back he'll——— me.
Pretty Bobby Shafto.

II

A diller, a dollar.
A two o'clock scholar.
What makes you——— so soon?
You used to———at two o'clock,
But now you——— at noon.

A long-married wife told her husband that he should experiment with eating her pussy, as she had heard it was a thrilling experience. The husband, who had never heard of such a thing, went manfully to the task. The taste wasn't bad but the smell was overpowering. Suddenly the wife orgasmed and, simultaneously, emitted a tremendous fart.

"Thank God," sighed the husband, "for a breath of fresh air!"

A novice nun was permitted to say only two words per year in the cloister of her particular order. Each year she did this in response to a question posed by the Mother Superior.

The first year the Mother Superior asked her, "How do you like it here, Sister?"

"Bad food," was the novice's reply.

At the end of the second year the Mother Superior asked her, "How do you like it here, Sister?"

"Poor company," was the terse reply.

At the end of the third year, the Mother Superior again asked her favorite question, but this time the novice nun replied: "I quit."

"I'm not surprised," said the Mother Superior. "You have been here three years now, Sister, and all you've done is bitch, bitch, bitch!"

An American traveling in the United Kingdom was riding in a British train compartment with an Englishman and an elderly English lady with her pet Pekinese.

They had traveled only a short distance when the dog threw up over the American's trousers.

Instead of apologizing, the Englishwoman fondled her dog and comforted it saying, "Poor itsy-bitsy doggie has a little tummy ache."

A few kilometers later the dog raised its leg and pissed all over the American's shoe.

Again the Englishwoman consoled her dog, saying, "Poor itsy-bitsy doggie has a cold in the bladder."

A short while later the dog shat all over the Yank's other shoe. Exasperated, the American stood up, grabbed the dog and threw it out of the window.

At this point the Englishman commented: "You Yanks are a peculiar lot. You speak the wrong language. You live on the wrong side of the ocean. And you, sir, threw the wrong bitch out of the window!"

John took his new girl to the movies, which they both enjoyed. After the show he asked what she wanted to do. "I want to get weighed," she said.

He took her to the drugstore, where the machine said her weight was 107 pounds.

Afterwards, she pouted and sulked for the rest of the evening.

When John finally escorted her home, he tried to kiss her at the door, but she pushed him away, saying, "Go on home. I had a wowsy time."

A sweet young thing marries an old man for his money. On their wedding night she jumps into bed and he holds up five fingers.

"Oh, honey," she said with delight, "does that mean five times?"

"No. You can pick one out."

The white missionary had lived in peace in the African village for more than a year but now, as the tribal Chief approached him, he knew there was a problem.

"What is it, Chief?" he asked.

"You in big trouble," the Chief said. "Yesterday white baby was born to my cousin. You only white man in village. We probably decide to roast you alive."

The missionary looked at the hillside behind the Chief. "Look, old man," he said. "I know it looks bad. But you see that flock of white sheep?"

"I see 'em."

"Then notice that black sheep in the flock. It's the only one and there are no other black sheep in the village."

"Okay, okay," said the Chief hastily. "You no tell and I no tell."

A man got into his berth on the train and started to fall asleep when he heard someone in the berth above him say, "Suck, Becky, suck! Blowing is just a figure of speech!"

Three women were boasting about their husbands.

One said, "My Cyrus is Secretary of State," and she proceeded to talk about Cyrus.

The second said, "My Bob is with the agriculture department," and talked about him.

The third said, "My husband Schenley—" and was interrupted by the first woman.

"But isn't Schenley a liquor?"

The third woman said, "You know my husband?"

The attractive wife told her husband she was going on vacation with a girlfriend, but she really went with her long-time wealthy lover, who gave her a beautiful $10,000 mink coat. But she couldn't bring it home so she figured a way. She pawned the mink coat.

She came home and told her husband she had found a pawn ticket, which was really the pawn ticket to her mink coat; and she asked her husband to find out what had been pawned.

Her husband returned and told his wife it was just a cheap watch. The next day his secretary was wearing a $10,000 mink coat.

Every morning, the crowd on Coney Island beach was startled to see a jogger with the build of a pro football player but a head the size of a baseball. Finally, some brave young man got up the nerve to stop him and ask, "What happened to give you such a small head?"

The jogger sadly told the story of finding a magic lamp on the beach, which produced a beautiful genie when rubbed. The genie said, "I now give you one wish. Do you want a quick fuck or a little head?"

The tall blonde model told the clerk: "I don't know the style or color of shoes, but I want low heels." The clerk asked, "To wear with what?" She said, "A short, plump, elderly dress manufacturer."

So this traveling salesman got an audience with the Pope.

"Hey, Father," he said. "Have you heard the joke about the two Polacks who—"

"My son," the Pope said. "I'm Polish."

The salesman thought for a minute. "That's okay, Father," he said. "I'll tell it very slowly."

young girl swallowed a pin when she was eleven and never felt a prick until she turned eighteen.

The on-the-make young executive drinking at the bar was taken aback when the pretty office worker he propositioned snapped at him: "No, buster, you've got the words 'liberated' and 'free' mixed up!"

Little Johnny was playing airplane with an orange crate.

"Here I am, a real US Army pilot, flying at 30,000 feet," he said to himself and made accompanying flight noises.

Little Mary got interested in what he was doing.

"Can I fly with you, Johnny?" she asked.

"Wait a minute," little Johnny said, as he cut back his engine sounds. "I'll bring her in like a real US Army pilot and then I'll take you up for a spin."

Little Mary climbed on the back of the orange crate.

"Fasten your seat belt," little Johnny commanded. "I'm a real US Army pilot, so prepare for take-off!" He ran through the check list and got airborne at last.

But at 30,000 feet little Mary announced that she had to pee.

"Don't scrub the mission just for that," little Johnny said amiably. "You've got to hang in there for a while yet!"

After a while he noticed a yellow stream between his feet. He glanced around and saw little Mary's snatch exposed.

"Gee that's cute," he said. "Can I touch it?"

She nodded, and he did so very briefly.

"Would you like to kiss it?" she asked.

"I'm not a *real* US Army pilot," little Johnny said.

Define the difference between a snake and a goose.

A snake is an asp in the grass, while a goose is a clasp. . . .

POEM

The Lapper reaps as he sows
With a Ph.D. tongue and a "69" pose.
This twot titillator is much in demand;
He cleans up the kitchen
And thinks that it's grand.

Q: What did Adam say to Eve on the moment that she first came on the scene?
A: You'd better stand back. I don't know how long it's gonna get.

Q: What did the elephant say when he saw the naked man lying on the ground?
A: How can he eat with that thing?

Hey, have you heard about the swell-looking lady sheriff from West Texas?"

"No. What about her?"

"She's got the biggest posse in El Puso."

A young coed, very pretty and sexy, wore an extra tight blouse and skirt which magnified her abundant charms.

She wriggled up to her professor after class and cooed: "Professor, I'd do anything to pass your exam with high marks."

The professor smiled at her, "Anything?"

"Yes, anything. . ."

"Okay," the professor said. "Study!"

A nosy neighbor remonstrated with the woman in the adjourning apartment. "Mrs. Smith, do you think it right that this seventeen-year-old boy spends three hours every night in your apartment?"

Mrs. Smith replied, "It's a platonic friendship. It's play for him and a tonic for me."

CENSORED SHAKESPEARE

I

What's in a name? That which we call a———
By any other name would smell as sweet.

II

You yourself
Are much condemned to have an itching———

III

Thou canst not say I did it; never shake
Thy gory——— at me.

The gynecologist complimented the young woman on his examination table. "Go home and tell your husband to prepare for a baby."

"But I don't have a husband," the girl replied.

"Then, go home and tell your lover."

"But I don't have a lover. I've never had a lover!"

"In that case," the doctor sighed, "go home and tell your mother to prepare for the second coming of Christ."

The well-proportioned black lady was doing her laundry outside on a warm August day in the heart of Alabama. Each time she rubbed downward on the scrubbing board her skirt hiked up over her naked ass.

A jackass looped up behind her and stuck its tongue into her crotch.

Without missing a stroke or even bothering to turn her head, she said: "I don't know who you are, but I does the washin' here every Tuesday and Thursday."

On an isolated part of a beach, a young boy and girl were teasing each other. They were boasting about how one had more than the other of everything.

The nine-year-old boy figured out a way to win the contest. He removed his swim trunks and said, "See, here's something you don't have."

The little girl ran away and returned a few minutes later. She pulled down the bottom of her bathing suit. "My mommy says that with one of these, I can get as many of those as I want."

What did the Polack do with his first fifty-cent piece?
He married her.

A guy walked into the confessional booth and confessed to the priest, "Father, I got laid ten times today!"

The shocked priest exclaimed, "What kind of Catholic are you?"

"I'm not a Catholic at all . . . but I had to tell someone!"

A tour bus traveling through northern Nevada paused briefly at the Mustang Ranch, near Sparks. The guide noted: "We are now passing the largest house of prostitution in America."

A male passenger piped up: "Why?"

Two girls were comparing their experiences at the company's annual Christmas party.

"Did you get laid, Helen?"

"Twice."

"Only twice?"

"Yeah, once by the band and once by the shipping room crew."

She had so many martinis during the party, that when the young virgin was deflowered in the back seat of the Cadillac, her boy friend said shyly, "Well babe, you've lost your olive."

comely young blonde was telling he friend at a cocktail party that she was off men for life. "They lie, they cheat, they are just no good. From now on, when I want sex I'll use my vibrator."

"But what if the batteries run out? What will you do?" asked the friend.

"Just what I do with my boy friend—I'll fake an orgasm."

Joanne was eagerly awaiting her blind date's arrival when the doorbell rang and rang. Alice, Joanne's roommate, peeked out the window at the date and let out a great shriek: "My God, you're in it for tonight, Joanne, he's ringing the bell from the bottom of the stairs."

Two girls decided to vacation in Miami Beach together. Neither suspected that the other was also a lesbian. The first night as they shared the same bed for the first time, one rolled over and whispered into her companion's ear, "Let me be frank . . ." at which point the other said soulfully, "No, let me be Frank . . . you can be John."

Alex came home from a business trip to Chicago and found no one home but his daughter Rose, who was crying bitterly.

"What's the matter, darling?" asked Alex.

"Mommy almost died last night," sobbed Rose.

"That's nonsense," said the father. "Why do you say that?"

"Well," said Rose, "you always told us that when we die we'll see God; so when I heard Mommy moaning last night I rushed to her bedroom and she was screaming, 'Oh God, here I come,' and she would have but Uncle Jerry held her down."

oris had the most beautiful breasts Don had ever seen. His desire to see them fully exposed was his number one passion. Finally he approached Doris and said, "I'll give you $100 if you'll take off your blouse and let me kiss your nipples." Doris, who was always broke, agreed and proceeded to take off her blouse and bra.

Don stared so hard that a wet spot suddenly blossomed on his trousers.

"Well, what are you waiting for?" asked Doris, "don't you have the nerve?"

"I don't have the $100," sighed Don.

Theresa and Jerry shacked up in a barn during a rainstorm. The screwing was so good that they decided to stay the night.

The next morning the farmer heard the commotion in the hayloft and entered his barn shouting, "What's going on in here?"

"We're living on the fruits of love," yelled Jerry.

"Well you better stop soon," said the farmer. "The skins are killing my chickens."

A woman waiting for a train weighed herself on a scale. A card came out with her weight and her fortune: "102 pounds—go over to track two and you'll get fucked."

Astonished but curious, she went over to track two and it actually happened! She was amazed that the scale could predict such a fortune so accurately.

She returned to track one and got on the scale a second time. A card came out with the same weight for her, but this time the fortune read: "Go over to track 12 and you'll fart."

She went over to track 12 and immediately farted several times in a row without any control over her body.

This time she ran back to the scale and got on it a third time. A card popped out with the exact same weight, but the fortune read:

"While you've been fucking and farting around, you missed your damn train!"

One of two gays who were living together suddenly fell in love with the handsome young doctor who had opened up his practice just across the street from their apartment.

"I'd just love to meet him," said one gay to his roommate, "if you have no objections. But I don't know how to go about it."

"I don't mind, sweets. Have your fling. It's easy to meet him. Just pose as one of his patients."

So the first one went to the doctor's office the next day and said his name was Mister Smith.

"What's your problem, Mr. Smith?" the doctor asked.

"Oh, doctor, I have such a terrible pain in my rectum."

"Let's have a look," said the doctor. "Take off your trousers and climb up on the table there."

"Gladly, doctor," lisped the patient eagerly.

The doctor parted his cheeks and looked up inside with a flashlight.

"Holy smoke!" the doctor exclaimed. "No wonder you have pains. Do you realize that you have one dozen American Beauty roses up in there?"

"Never mind the roses," the patient said. "Just read the card!"

A young nun said to her Mother Superior:

"I was out walking in the garden last night and the gardener took me, threw me to the ground and, well, you know . . . Can you give me penance?"

"Go and eat ten lemons," said the Mother Superior.

"But that won't cleanse my sins away."

"I know, but it will wipe that contented grin off your face."

An American, an Englishman, and a Frenchman were discussing a good example of savoir-faire.

"Well," said the American, "if you came home and found your wife in bed with another man and you didn't kill the son of a bitch, that to me is savoir-faire."

"Not quite, chaps," said the Englishman. "If you came home and found your wife in bed with another man and you said, 'Please, sir, carry on,' that's savior-faire."

"Mais non," said the Frenchman. "If you came home and found your wife in bed with another man and you said, 'Please, sir, carry on' and the man was able to continue, *he's* got savoir-faire!"

On a town beside an Indian reservation a beautiful Indian girl was soliciting business, when a prospect asked her rate.

"One hundred dollars!" he exclaimed. "Why, the Indians sold Manhattan for only twenty-four dollars."

"Could be," she smiled and wiggled her hips. "But Manhattan just lies there."

One evening after attending the theater, two gentlemen were walking down the street when they observed a well-dressed, attractive young lady walking just ahead of them. One turned to the other and said, "I'd give fifty bucks to spend the night with that woman." To their surprise, the woman turned and said, "I'll take you up on that." She had a neat appearance and a pleasant voice, so after bidding his friend goodnight the man accompanied the lady to her apartment, where they immediately went to bed.

The following morning the man presented her with twenty-five dollars as he prepared to leave. She demanded the rest of the money, stating, "If you don't give me the other twenty-five I'll sue you for it." He laughed, saying, "I'd like to see you get it on these grounds."

The next day he was surprised when served with a summons ordering his presence in court as defendant. He hurried to his lawyer and explained the details of the case. His lawyer said, "She can't possibly get a judgment against you on such grounds, but it will be interesting to see how her case will be presented."

After the usual preliminaries. the lady's lawyer ad dressed the court as follows:

"Your Honor, my client is the owner of a piece of property, a garden spot surrounded by a profuse growth of shrubbery, which property she agreed to rent to the defendant for a specified length of time for the sum of fifty dollars. The defendant took possession of the property, used it extensively for the purpose for which it was rented, but upon evacuating the premises he paid only twenty-five dollars. The rent is not excessive since it was restricted property, and we ask judgment to be granted against the defendant to assure payment of the balance."

The defendant's lawyer was impressed and amused at the way the case had been presented. His defense was therefore somewhat altered from what he had planned. "Your Honor, my client agrees the young lady has a fine piece of property, for a degree of pleasure was derived from the transaction. However, my client found a well on the property, around which he placed his own stones, sunk a shaft and erected a pump, all labor being personally performed by him. We claim these improvements to the property are sufficient to offset the unpaid balance, and that the plaintiff was adequately compensated for the rental of the said property. We therefore ask that the judgment not be granted."

The young lady's lawyer's comeback was this: "Your Honor, my client agrees that the defendant did find a well on the property, and he did make improvements such as described by my opponent; however, had the defendant not known the well existed, he would never have rented the property; also, on evacuating the premises, the defendant moved the stones, pulled out the shaft and took the pump with him. In so doing he not only dragged his equipment through the shrubbery, but left the hole much larger than it was prior to his occupancy, making it easily accessible to little children. We therefore ask judgment be granted."

(She Got It)